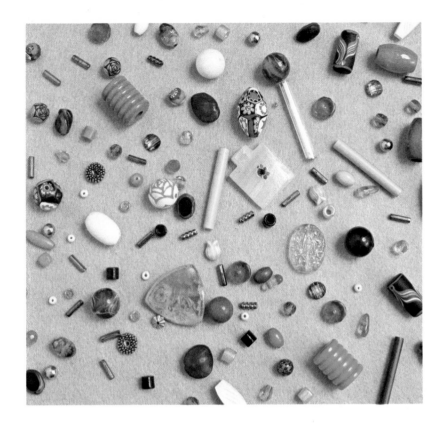

STEP-BY-STEP
BEADCRAFT

By Judith Glassman

 **Golden Press • New York**
Western Publishing Company, Inc.
Racine, Wisconsin

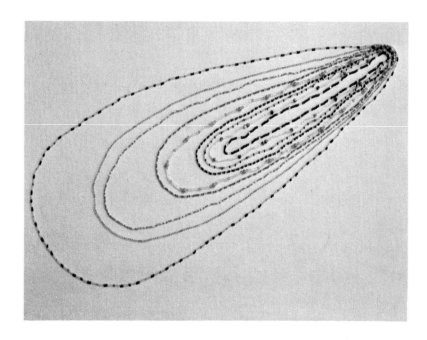

Art Director: Remo Cosentino
Art Assistants: Barbara Braunstein,
                  Elizabeth Alexander
Diagrams: Gary Tong
Editor: Caroline Greenberg
Photographs: George Ancona

Library of Congress Catalog Card Number: 73–88437

Contents

Introduction 4

Materials and Equipment 9
   Beads 9
   Needles 10
   Thread 13
   Looms 13
   Findings 14
   Miscellaneous 14

Work and Storage Methods 15

Making Beads 16
   Clay Beads 16
   Corn Starch Beads 17
   Cloth, Felt, or Paper Beads 17
   Scented Rose Beads 17

Beads From Nature 18

Finishing Beaded Pieces 19
   Knotted Closings 19
   Findings 19
   Miscellaneous Closings 20
   Ending Loomed Beadwork 20

Basic Bead Necklace and Variations 23

Seed Bead Daisy Necklace 25

Chevron Belt 26

Braided Necklace 27

Loop Necklace 29

Primitive Pendant 30

Two-Needle Beading 31
   Classic Eye Necklace 31
   Two-Needle Choker 33
   Star Pattern Choker 34
   Bamboo Necklace 35

Bibs 36

Mexican Lace 39
   Technique and Sampler 39
   Mexican Lace Window Hanging 40

Wire and Beads 41
   Beaded Ring 41
   Wire Choker 41
   Wire Bracelet 42

Bead Looms 43
   Making a Loom 44
   Loomed Belt 46
   Bracelets and Headbands 48
   Loomed Choker 49
   Indian Loomed Necklace With Fringe 51

Bead Weaving Without a Loom 52
   Even Row (One-Needle) Technique 52
      Technique and Sampler 52
      Peyote Belt 53
   Odd Row (Two-Needle) Technique 54

Bead Embroidery 55
   One-Needle Method 55
   Two-Needle Method 56
   Patterns 56

Macramé, Knitting, and Crochet 57
   Macramé Wind Chimes 57
   Knitting Technique 59
      Knit Purse 59
   Crocheting With Beads 61

Beads and Chain 62
   Simple Bead and Chain Necklace 62
   Four-Bead Necklace 63
   Beaded Earrings 63

Bibliography and Suppliers 64

Introduction

(Below) Egyptian collar of faïence beads, late eighteenth dynasty. The Metropolitan Museum of Art, Rogers Fund, 1940. (Below left) Egyptian ceramic beads from the eleventh dynasty. The Metropolitan Museum of Art, Gift of Miss Helen Miller Gould, 1910. (Below right) Bracelets and anklets from the twelfth dynasty. The Metropolitan Museum of Art, contribution from Henry Walters and the Rogers Fund, 1916.

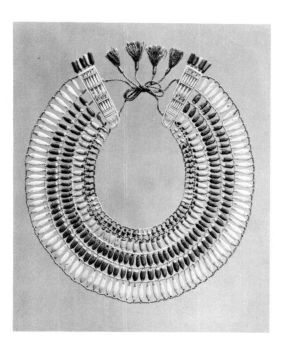

Who was the first man to pick up a shell or a hollow bone or an animal's tooth and transform it into a piece of personal adornment? Whoever he was, he was an ancient man, for the history of beads and beading is almost as old as the human race. Plant seeds were probably used as the first beads, and from as early as 30,000 B.C. men were piercing shells, teeth, and bone and stringing them into collars, necklaces, and other decorations. Stone Age skeletons wearing elaborate beaded headdresses have been unearthed by archaeologists. In ancient Egypt beadmaking reached its greatest period during the twelfth dynasty (1991–1786 B.C.), when the art of making faïence, or glazed pottery, beads was at its height. Glass beads were made in Egypt as early as the fifth century B.C.

Beads have been associated with religion and superstition throughout the ages. Buddhists were probably the first to use beads to help them count their prayers. Christians and Moslems also use them for that purpose. The word bead itself is derived from the English word *bede*, meaning prayer. Bedesmen or bedeswomen were professionals whose job it was to offer up prayers for other people. Soon the word came to be associated with the beads used to count these prayers.

Many kinds of beads were thought to have special powers. Red coral beads were travelers' talismans in Greece and Rome; amber beads were thought of as healers; large cobalt-blue ceramic "donkey beads" are thought by Middle Easterners to bring good luck; and large beads strung on leather thongs, called "worrybeads," get clicked around in the fingers of modern Greeks (the rhythmic motion is relaxing, and so thought to give the habit a therapeutic value).

(Left) Beaded crown, Yoruba Tribe, Nigeria. Done in brilliantly colored E beads, using several different beading techniques. Harry Franklin Gallery, Beverly Hills.

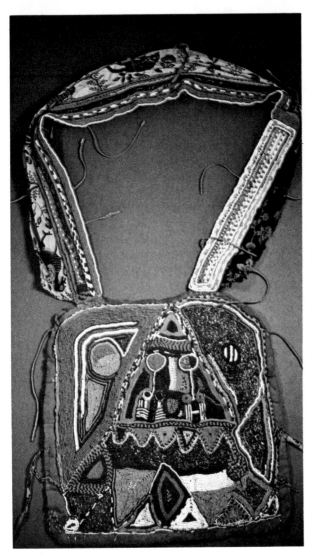

(Left) Beaded chief's ritual apron, Yoruba Tribe, Nigeria. (Above) Detail, showing the arrangement of beads used to create the dense and varied texture. Collection of Mr. and Mrs. Harry Franklin, Beverly Hills.

American Indian bead embroidery with the lazy stitch used as a background (see page 55). Owned by Douglas Johnson, San Francisco. Photo by George Glassman, New York.

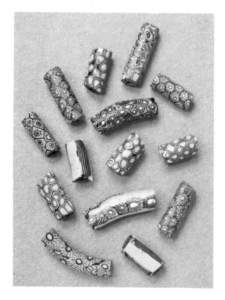

Intricately patterned African trade beads like these are avidly collected today.

Beads have been used by many peoples as a form of communication. American Indian seed bead items, including vests, moccasins, belts, leg bands, saddlebags, knife sheaths, yokes, headbands and hatbands, contain symbolic designs that tell stories or commemorate events. Many African tribes also use beads to send messages, even for missives as complicated as love letters. And there is certainly a form of exuberant communication in the beaded necklaces, called "throws," that get tossed from person to person in New Orleans at Mardi Gras, and in Rio de Janeiro at Carnival.

Beads have played even more important roles in world history, however. They are commonly used for barter among primitive societies. Wampum, the American Indian's coin of the realm, was made of shells. These shells, which were naturally white, were dyed purple or black for different values. They were strung into chains, woven into belts, or embroidered onto fabric. They were used as money, both among the Indians themselves and between Indians and European settlers. Wampum was used until the eighteenth century, when machines began producing it, resulting in disastrous inflation.

The discovery of the trade value of beads led to their use by European explorers. They found that beads were as attractive to African tribes as they were to native Americans, and could be exchanged for goods, supplies, or information. Bead trading in Africa was quite complex, however. Certain tribes would only accept certain kinds of beads for trade, and the success or failure of an expedition could depend on whether or not the right beads were available in the right amounts. When the journalist Henry M. Stanley set out to find David Livingstone he left an entry in his journal about how appalled he was at the number and variety of beads he had to carry. Evidently, he carried enough.

Glass beads were produced in Europe from as early as the thirteenth century. They were made by glassblowers who began with bubbles of glass that they then blew into long tubes. These hollow tubes were stretched into long rods and were then cut, tumbled, and polished. Color was either in the glass as it was blown or was added afterward. Venice was the center of bead-making for quite a long time, but there were large beadmaking industries in England and Amsterdam during the sixteenth and seventeenth centuries, and America counted beadmaking as one of its first important industries as well.

Beading as a craft has long been overshadowed by the importance of commercial beading. At the turn of the century, when proper Victorian ladies were very much attached to their beaded bags (done with the tiniest beads imaginable), beading involved hideous sweatshop labor. In 1906 these conditions were exposed by the Women's Industrial Council in an exhibition, held in London, called The Daily News Sweated Industries Exhibition.

Beaded bag, dated 1827, but probably made much later. From the collection of Diana Finegold.

(Right) The triangular beads in this blue plastic 1930s necklace have holes at the bottom and the top. (Below) A 1920s pendant with fringe combines pale pink glass beads with crystal and metal.

Interest in beading undergoes periodic revivals. The great beading craze that swept America in the 1960s was a result of new interest in the American Indian, whose exquisite beaded articles had long been neglected by all but collectors. Today's interest in beading combines a continuing fascination with natural materials (feathers, shells, abalone, stones, seeds, bone) and a revived awareness of the plastics used in the 1920s and the 1930s.

Most beads today are made in Europe in modern factories. They are used extensively by clothing manufacturers and are available in new styles every season, just like clothes or cars.

Beading is a craft with links to the past that are strong and satisfying. You need only see some of the exquisite beaded museum pieces to realize the range of expressive possibilities inherent in beads. In addition to being used to make all kinds of jewelry, beads can be embroidered on clothing, used for wall or window hangings, strung to make curtains or room dividers, woven into place mats or trivets. They can be used in conjunction with knitting, crocheting, or macramé. Beadcraft can be as simple as a single-strand necklace or it can be as complicated as a wide seed-bead belt made from an intricate graphed pattern.

This book contains many beading projects, ranging from the most basic to the highly complex. It also contains suggestions for working with beads that I have found useful. Take these suggestions as starting points, not hard and fast rules. Experiment on your own and keep notes, especially of items you give away or sell. Work with color, texture, size, and shape. Whatever is an expression of your sensibility will make the most beautiful beaded works.

Materials and Equipment

Beads

If you think beads are *all* of the Indian seed variety, you're in for a surprise. Beads come in all materials, shapes, and sizes. Beads can be so small they're measured in millimeters (mm) or they can be over 5 inches long. They can be made of plastic, glass, crystal, wood, cork, metal, bone, shell, bamboo, porcelain, clay, jade, coral, garnet, pearl, opal, or of many other materials. Anyone with a mind to can also make them out of paper, leather, pasta, empty thread spools, roses, seeds, or such items as keys and buttons. Beads can be found in attics and old trunks, at antique shows, auctions, and garage sales. They can be scavenged from old beaded bags, clothing, necklaces, and so on. The list is endless.

Seed beads, the smallest beads available, are round outside and inside. They are made of plastic, glass, or metal. *Rocailles* are the same size as seed beads, are round outside, and have square holes. (Rocailles can be substituted for seed beads.) *Bugle beads* are the same diameter as seed beads but are longer. *E beads* are about three times as big as seed beads.

Seed beads are sold almost everywhere these days, but they're likely to come in small packages and you'll probably pay a lot more per bead for them sold that way than you would if you bought them from a store specializing in beads. They are also available in some retail outlets in cellophane packages or strung

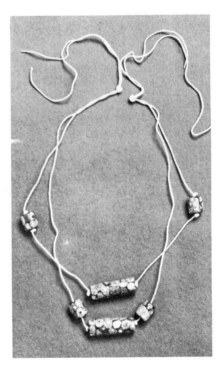

(Above) Matte finish millefiore beads strung on heavy white crochet cotton. (Left) Seed beads in cellophane package, tube, and plastic blister pack, and in a kilo (2.2 pounds) bunch.

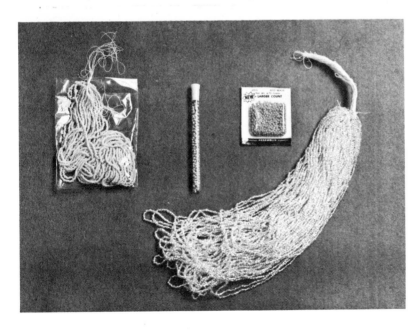

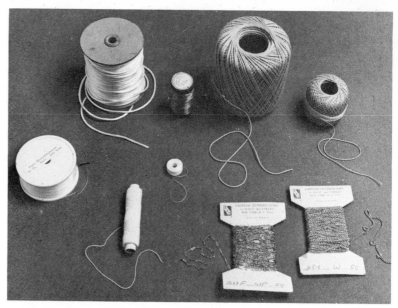

Clockwise, from upper right: Two different kinds of crochet cotton, two kinds of chain, nylon beading thread (multifilament), elastic, monofilament, rattail, and wire.

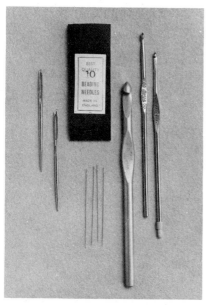

Needles used for beading range from heavy tapestry needles to the finest needles for seed beads. Various crochet hooks can be used when crocheting with beads.

in bunches of about 1000. Many beading outlets are listed on page 64. Some of them sell *only* wholesale, meaning they sell seed beads by the kilo (2.2 pounds), larger beads by the "masse" (about 1200 beads).

Larger beads are also sold wholesale. Many wooden beads under 8 mm in size are strung in bunches of 10 strings or 1000 beads each. Larger beads are sold by the hundred or by the dozen. Some large, expensive beads are sold individually. If you know where to go, you can buy a lot of beads for, say, five dollars.

Needles

For seed beads you'll need special very thin, very small-eyed beading needles which are sold six to a pack. They can be frustrating to thread when you first start using them. The holes in regular sewing needles look enormous in comparison. A threader is included in the package, but that usually breaks the first time you use it. Persevere in a good light and you'll soon discover how best to do it yourself.

Larger beads do not require a special beading needle. You can thread them with ordinary sewing needles. In some cases, when you use a thicker type of thread, a yarn needle is called for. Sometimes you may want to stiffen the end of your thread with glue and use no needle at all.

If you make your own beads (see page 16), you may need a darning needle, a tapestry needle, or a toothpick to pierce them.

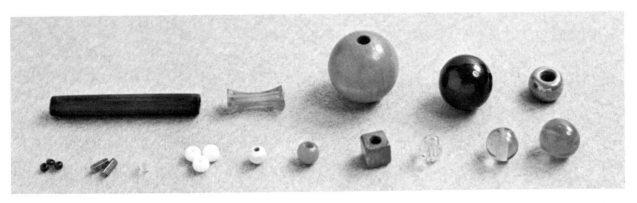

(Above) Top row, left to right: 1½″ tube, ½″ tube, 16-mm round, 12-mm round, pony bead. Bottom row, right to left: 9-mm round, 8-mm round, 6-mm crystal, 5-mm cube, 5-mm round, 4-mm round, E beads, 3-mm round, bugles, seed beads. (Below) An efficient plastic storage box, showing an assortment of beads.

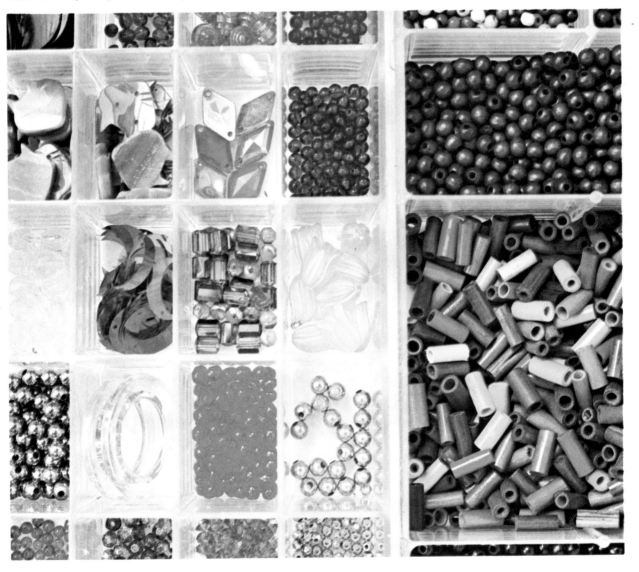

Necklace by Kasoundra can be worn in many ways. Owned by Anita Sanders.

Thread

For seed beads, lightweight nylon monofilament (about 12 gauge) is good to use. You can also use a special nylon beading thread, thin but very strong, that is sold in some beading outlets. Dental floss can also be used for small beads.

Carpet thread, buttonhole thread, embroidery cotton, and heavier gauge monofilament are good for medium-sized beads, and you can use anything you want for really big beads: yarns, slippery rayon rattail, textured soutache, and so on. Interesting effects can be obtained by combining large beads with different kinds and textures of yarn. Macramé, knitting, and crocheting combine well with large beads.

You can achieve special effects by using 25 to 28 gauge wire. Thin elastic, available at notions counters, can be useful for bracelets, chokers, headbands, and belts. Chain can be used very effectively with beads to make beautiful jewelry, too.

Beeswax will give any fibrous thread more body, will help beads move smoothly, and may help your finished work last longer. To wax your thread, just pull it over a piece of wax.

Looms

For certain projects a loom is necessary. The one pictured here is fairly standard, but if you're making something that's longer than 4 or 5 inches you'll have to keep unrolling and rewinding your work. This can break your work rhythm, and so, on page 44, there are instructions for building your own loom. This type will enable you to work continuously on much longer pieces.

A standard beading loom

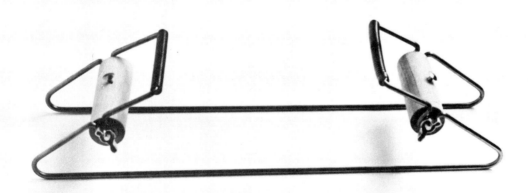

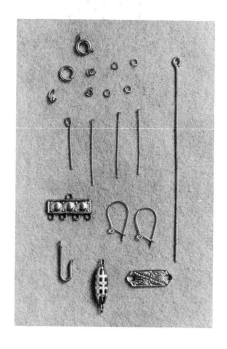

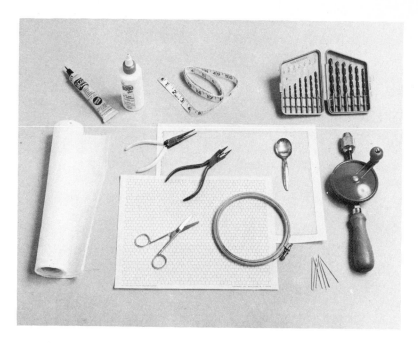

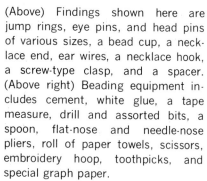

(Above) Findings shown here are jump rings, eye pins, and head pins of various sizes, a bead cup, a necklace end, ear wires, a necklace hook, a screw-type clasp, and a spacer. (Above right) Beading equipment includes cement, white glue, a tape measure, drill and assorted bits, a spoon, flat-nose and needle-nose pliers, roll of paper towels, scissors, embroidery hoop, toothpicks, and special graph paper.

Findings

You can give your work a professional finish by using manufactured pieces for jewelry called findings. These include fastenings, such as spring rings and hooks; jewelry endings, such as bead cups and necklace ends; and jewelry attachments, such as jump rings, eye pins, and head pins. Some of the findings you may need are illustrated here; others will be discussed within specific projects.

Miscellaneous

You will need a pair of scissors, a ruler or tape measure, a pair of needle-nose pliers (with built-in wire cutters), and some kind of fast-drying, colorless glue. (In this book, materials for projects requiring glue call for jewelers' cement, but epoxy and white glue are also suitable.)

Toothpicks are useful for applying dabs of cement to small places, and paper towels or a damp sponge are good to have handy for cleaning up glue mishaps. A small spoon is more practical than fingers for dipping into bead containers. If you bead with seashells, nut shells, or stones, you may need a drill or an awl to pierce them. For some pieces, such as wall or window hangings, you will need dowels. You'll need special graph paper (see page 45) to plan designs for loom work, and an embroidery hoop for sewing with beads. If your light source isn't good enough, you'll be the first to know.

Work and Storage Methods

If your beading fervor is in its early stages, you should be able to find enough bottles and jars in which to store your beads securely and display them attractively. If your passion starts to grow beyond normal bounds—and it probably will—you'll find yourself looking for function rather than beauty. I've found that compartmented plastic boxes are invaluable. They come in several sizes, and different models have different numbers and arrangements of compartments. Some styles are suitable for seed beads, some for larger beads. They are transparent, and, when new, shiny and attractive. They do scratch easily, and after a while become lackluster. But they *are* practical.

To work, take some beads out of their containers and put them on your work surface. Some people like to work from plates, ashtrays, or jar tops. I find pieces of felt or plain paper, a separate piece for each color or kind of bead, to be best. Felt is particularly good for round beads, as they roll less on felt than on paper. When you've finished working, it's an easy matter to funnel all the beads back into storage without losing any. (And anyone who has tried to bead with a small child in the house knows the importance of being able to clean up quickly.)

Beading does not require a lot of space, and you can easily devise a work surface that is portable.

Making Beads

The advantages of making your own beads are obvious. You can create your own shapes, sizes, textures, and colors—even odors—out of a wide variety of materials.

Clay Beads

Clay beads can be made from Kaolin, a very pure white clay, but such beads are hard to glaze and you'll have more interesting results with less effort if you use the clay product known as Egyptian paste. Egyptian paste contains a glaze in the mixture so no separate firing is necessary. It can have either a matte or a shiny finish, depending on the firing temperature used. Matte finish beads will not stick together and can be fired in a Pyrex or other heat-proof bowl. Shiny Egyptian paste beads must be separated and strung on nichrome wire when they are fired.

To make beads, work the clay into balls, tubes, loops—anything that, with a hole, can be strung. Make score marks with a fork, leave smooth, or texture with terry cloth, sandpaper, pebbles, etc. Pierce with a tapestry needle and fire in kiln according to instructions on the package.

(Above) Note the texturing on these chunky ceramic beads, strung on red rattail. (Right) Egyptian paste beads: matte finish on the left, glossy finish on the right. These necklaces use traditionally shaped beads as well as freer, more imaginative shapes. All three by Sheila Geist.

Corn Starch Beads

1 cup corn starch
2 cups baking soda
1¼ cups cold water

Blend corn starch and baking soda. Add water and mix until smooth. Cook over medium heat, stirring constantly, until mixture is the consistency of mashed potatoes. Remove from heat and cover with a damp cloth until cooled. Knead thoroughly. Add a few drops of food coloring if desired. Shape into bead shapes and pierce with a toothpick. Allow beads to dry for 24 to 48 hours, then paint, if desired. Seal with shellac or clear nail polish.

Cloth, Felt, or Paper Beads

Cut out shapes like those shown (or larger), roll snugly around a darning needle, and glue at the end. Longer versions of the same shapes can be wrapped around knitting needles of different thicknesses.

Scented Rose Beads

Tear petals off fresh roses and chop them fine. Put them in an iron pot and add a little water, just enough to barely cover the petals. Heat very gently for about an hour, or until the mixture is gummy. Do *not* boil. Roll small pieces of the pulpy mixture into balls and let dry in the open. Pierce and thread the beads, using a heavy needle that has been heated. Since it may take a few days for the beads to dry completely, move them back and forth on the thread from time to time to keep the holes open.

(Above left) Corn starch beads can be fanciful or plain; food colors can be mixed evenly throughout or marbled. (Above) Slick magazines provide colorful materials for paper beads. Interesting fabrics work well, too.

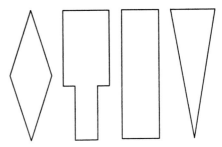

Some paper bead shapes

Beads From Nature

Seeds, feathers, some beans and peas, nut shells, seashells, stones—these are all potential beads. All you need to know is the proper technique for making holes in them.

Fresh fruit seeds are often soft enough to be pierced with a sharp needle. Clean and dry them first, then pierce with a threaded needle and slide them down the thread. Beans that have hard shells, like coffee beans, must be soaked in hot water until they are soft enough to be pierced.

Seashells, nut shells, and stones must be pierced either with a drill (use the finest bit—carbide for stone—and brace the item well) or an awl. Experiment with easy-to-get shells until you are satisfied that your technique is good. To protect delicate seashells while they are being drilled, cover the area to be drilled with masking tape.

The quills of feathers are hollow, or, if you want them to hang vertically, can be easily pierced.

If you live in a large city, you can buy feathers and shells, with ready-made holes, from a bead supply store.

Glass and wood and some metals can be used effectively with natural beads, but for esthetic reasons, jewelry made with natural beads should not be closed with jump rings or other jewelry findings. The natural look of the piece should be maintained throughout.

(Right) Necklace of shells, feathers, abalone, and bone. (Above) Detail of necklace showing closing. A tail of bone and abalone beads gets pulled through a loop of bone beads.

Finishing Beaded Pieces

Here are some basic finishing methods that will be useful in a variety of situations—to conceal the ends of thread or selvages, or to hold your pieces closed.

Knotted Closings

Knotted closings can be used for necklaces that are large enough to slip on over your head.

If you're using a needle and fibrous thread, tie the ends (two or four, depending on whether your thread is doubled) in a square knot. Pull taut. Place a dab of jewelers' cement on the knot. (If your thread is heavy, squeeze a bit of cement into the knot, too.) Draw the end with the needle back through two or three beads, and knot the end around the beaded thread, between beads. Pull taut. Place a dab of cement at this knot (use a toothpick), run the thread through two or more beads, pull taut, and cut the thread. Repeat with the remaining threads, running half through one side of the necklace and half through the other.

Use this running back and knotting technique to end off any thread in any type of beadwork. Anchor a new thread in the same way.

If you're using lightweight monofilament, make a square knot, dab some jewelers' cement on the knot, and make another knot over it. With a heavier gauge monofilament, hold a match near the knot to fuse it. Clip ends.

Findings

Another way of closing necklaces, bracelets, and belts is to use jewelers' findings. Bead cups, for instance, are used to conceal thread ends. Pass the thread ends through the hole in the bead cup and knot the thread a few times, keeping the bead cup as close as possible to the end of your piece. You may need to open the hooked part of the bead cup with pliers to give yourself room to work. When your knot is large enough so it won't slip back through the hole, cover it with jewelers' cement and let dry. Cut the thread end close to the knot and attach the bead cup to a jump ring. Press the hook of the bead cup closed.

When you are working on a necklace with a number of strands, you can use a necklace end. Necklace ends are findings with one or more holes on one side (for attaching one or more strands of beadwork or chain) and one hole on the other side (for attachment to a jump ring, hook, or other kind of clasp).

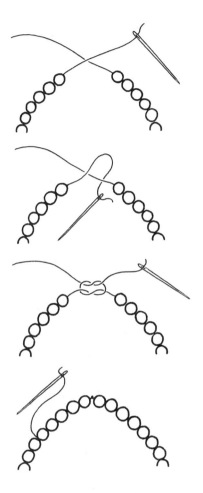

Simple knotted closing

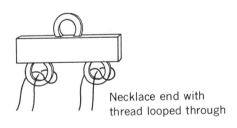

Necklace end with thread looped through

Bead cup with knot

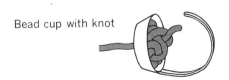

 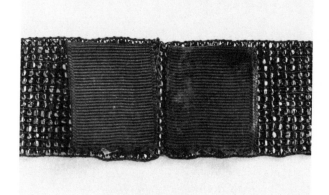

(Above) Closure using a circle of beads, from the Bamboo Necklace on page 35. (Above right) Close-up of selvage ending on a loomed piece (see page 48).

Loop one thread through a hole, pull close to the work, and pass the thread back through two or more beads. Knot and cement, as for finishing a necklace large enough to slip over your head. Repeat this procedure with each thread end.

Adjustable closings, good for ending chokers, require a tail of some sort on one end of the piece and a hook on the other. You can make the tail by alternating large and small beads at the beginning of the piece, as described in the instructions for the Star Pattern Choker, page 34. You can make another kind of tail by making a series of small circles, as described in the instructions for the Bamboo Necklace on page 35. In both methods, the hook is attached to the appropriate finding at the other end of the necklace.

If you are working with a single-strand necklace, you can attach each end to a jump ring by looping the thread around the jump ring and back into the work, as with the necklace end. Attach one of the jump rings to a spring ring, or to one of the other kinds of clasps you find at the findings' suppliers listed on page 64.

Miscellaneous Closings

Sometimes other types of closings are necessary. For the necklace on page 18, I wanted a closing that did not bring extraneous elements into the piece. I made a triangular hole at one end of the necklace by stringing three pieces of bone and then going back through the first piece. I finished the other end of the necklace with a tail of alternating bone beads and abalone triangles. When the necklace is worn, the tail gets pulled through the opening and holds there. The wire choker and bracelet (pages 41–42) are closed by hooking one end through a bead loop on the other end.

Loomed beadwork can be ended off in a number of ways. You

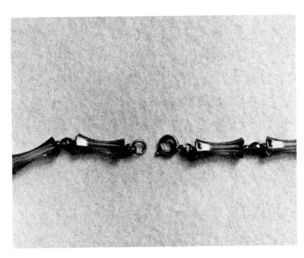

can cut your work from the loom, leaving your warp threads long enough so that each one can be woven and knotted back into the work, but I find this tedious—and also find that it distorts the work at the ends. It is simpler to make a selvage by running the weft thread over and under the warp threads for half an inch while the work is still on the loom. Cover this selvage with a thin layer of cement, let dry, and cut from the loom. If your ends are going to be loose (not closed, as they would be in an elastic bracelet, for instance), this selvage can be folded against the back of the work and a piece of ribbon cemented or sewn on to cover it. This piece of ribbon can be long enough to be used as a tie or, if you are using a buckle or some other closing, can just be decorative.

Other ties can be made from strips of appropriate cloth, rope, leather, crocheting, knitting, or macramé. Sew, crochet, or cement them to the ends of your piece. If you wish, you may sew or cement the entire work to a length of material. This will give added strength to the piece as well. Leave ends long enough to tie.

Another popular method of ending loomed work is the button and loop method. Starting an inch or so in from one end of your work, weave and knot a threaded needle through so that it comes out at the top corner. String enough beads on the thread to make a loop one-third the width of the piece. Weave the thread through the second third of the end row of beads. Make a second loop to cover the last third of the end row. If your work is very wide, make more loops; if very narrow, you may need only one. Weave and knot the thread back through the work to end off. Sew buttons or large beads to the other end of the work in positions to correspond to the loops.

See Bracelets and Headbands on page 48 for closure instructions if the ends of a piece are to be joined together.

(Above left) Buttons and loops used to close Peyote Belt (see page 53). (Above) Spring ring and jump ring closure on Loop Necklace (see page 29).

Three simple beaded necklaces: a long chain of 8-mm beads alternating with sections of seed beads, a brass and crystal choker strung on elastic thread, and a glass and seed bead necklace with an old clasp.

Basic Bead Necklace and Variations

Materials
2 strings (total) seed beads, seed beads and bugles, or any other combination
1 yard nylon monofilament *or* 2 yards nylon beading thread, carpet thread, or buttonhole thread
Beading needle
Jewelers' cement

Thread the needle, and if you're using a fibrous thread, wax and double it. If you're using monofilament, simply begin beading.

Thread one bead, push it down the thread, and go through it again in the same direction, leaving a 6-inch tail. This anchored bead will keep the other beads from slipping off the thread as you work. String beads in any pattern you desire: light and dark beads, transparent and opaque, in any arrangement of colors, sizes, shapes. Glass beads combined with wood make an arresting combination. Punctuate smooth lengths of bugle beads with large textured beads. Subtle variations in size can create their own texture.

Anchoring the first bead

To finish: When your necklace is long enough, end off as follows. *If your thread is doubled,* cut it from the needle as close to the eye as possible. Slip off the end bead (the one that served as an anchor) and discard. Tie all four ends in a square knot. Pull taut. Place a dab of jewelers' cement on the knot. Thread a needle with one of the ends; go through two beads, knot around thread, pull taut, dab with cement, go through two more beads, pull taut, and cut. Repeat with the other three ends.

If you're using monofilament, make a square knot, pull taut, dab with jewelers' cement, then make another knot directly over the first and pull taut. If you're using a heavy gauge monofilament, grasp the necklace with a needle-nose pliers, very carefully hold a match near the knot to fuse it, and cut the ends at the point of fusion. (This can be tricky, so don't attempt it on a fabulous piece of work until you've practiced with monofilament and match alone.)

A simple pendant made of old glass, crystal, and brass beads.

Variations

Pendants at the bottom of seed bead necklaces are an easy way to add interest. The technique couldn't be simpler. When your necklace is half as long as you want it to be, add one bead, then start adding beads in your pendant pattern. When the pendant is finished, go back through the top bead and continue the necklace.

If you have designed a pendant that requires two-needle beading (see page 31), start your necklace with the pendant, centering it on the thread. When the pendant is completed, separate the strands and finish the necklace, one strand at a time.

A pendant can be a simple loop, or loops within loops, cross pieces within loops, and so on.

Plain necklaces can be further embellished along their length by adding loops as you go. You can fringe the bottom of a necklace by adding six or seven beads, going around the seventh bead and back through the other six. Do this four or five times for a simple fringe at the bottom of a necklace, or fringe the whole necklace by making a fringe between every third or fourth bead along the whole length of the piece. Make necklaces with two or three separate strands instead of one. Anything goes!

Seed Bead Daisy Necklace

Materials

½ bunch white seed beads
½ string red seed beads
½ string yellow seed beads
½ string orange seed beads
3 yards beading thread
Beading needle
Jewelers' cement

Thread needle and double thread. String one white bead and go through the bead again to secure it, leaving 6 inches of thread at the end. String ten white beads.

String eight red beads. Go back through the first red bead. String one white bead for the center of the daisy, then go through the fifth red bead strung to form daisy. Make sure the daisy is pulled tight against the white beads.

Add ten more white beads and make a yellow daisy. Add another ten white beads and make an orange daisy. Continue in this way, alternating red, yellow, and orange daisies, until necklace is long enough to slip over your head.

Finish as for Basic Bead Necklace (see page 23).

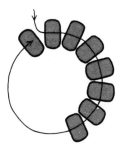

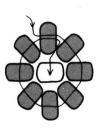

Forming a daisy

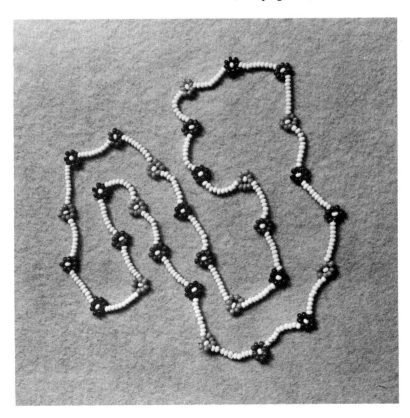

This Daisy Necklace is traditionally made of seed beads, but would be interesting made with larger beads as well.

start here

Chevron Belt

Materials

200 5-mm beveled cube wooden beads, color A
200 5-mm beveled cube wooden beads, color B
100 yards Speed-Cro-Sheen crochet thread in matching or contrasting color
#7 yarn needle

The belt shown here was made with four beads in the V of the chevron and three along the sides. Chevron chains can be made with other combinations of beads in the same proportions: five and four, six and five, etc., depending on how wide you want the finished piece to be.

String seven beads of color A, leaving an end of about 5 inches. String three beads of color B. Go back through the first four beads of color A. String three beads of color B. String three beads of color A and go through the seventh bead of color A. *String three beads of color B. String three beads of color A. Go through the fourteenth bead (color A).*

Repeat the steps between *, going through the last bead of the previous V each time you string three of color A. Continue until the chain is of desired length. Crochet the belt ties of Speed-Cro-Sheen and attach with slip stitches between beads on each end row.

Threading for Chevron Belt. Color A: dark beads. Color B: light beads.

The ties on this Chevron Belt were crocheted on a #0 crochet hook in a pattern that echoes the chevrons in the belt.

Braided Necklace

Materials

3 bunches seed beads in three different colors
18 yards beading thread
2 beading needles
2 necklace ends, 3-holed
2 jump rings
Spring ring
Piece of heavy cardboard
Jewelers' cement

Cut six pieces of thread, each 3 yards long. Pass one piece through an end hole in one of the necklace ends. Pass the other end of the same thread through the same hole in the opposite direction, making sure ends are equal, and pull tight. String each end of this thread with beads of one color, leaving an end of 3 inches. Loop thread around the last bead so that the beads don't slide off. Loop a second 3-yard length of thread through the same hole in the necklace end and repeat the stringing of beads.

Loop and bead the remaining four threads in the same way, arranging colors in any manner you wish. When you're finished, you should have four beaded strands emerging from each necklace-end hole.

Pin the necklace end to a piece of cardboard. Braid by holding the two left-most strands together and weaving them over and under every two strands of beads to the right, being careful to keep the strands flat and untwisted. When you have woven the first two strands all the way over to the right, repeat the weaving with the double strand that is now at the left. Continue in this manner until necklace is of desired length.

When the strands have been braided to the last bead, unloop the last beads in each strand and add or subtract beads so that the length of each beaded thread is the same. Put a needle on the left-most thread and loop it through the corresponding hole in the second necklace end. Pass the thread back through a couple of beads, knot, pass through two more beads, knot again, dot the thread with cement, pass through two more beads, pull taut, and cut the thread. Repeat with each thread. Attach one jump ring to the single hole of each necklace end; attach the spring ring to one of the jump rings. (This necklace is pictured on the following page.)

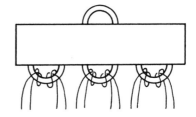

Threads looped around necklace end

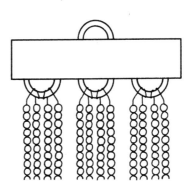

Beads strung

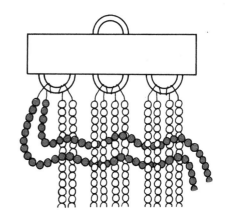

Beginning of braiding

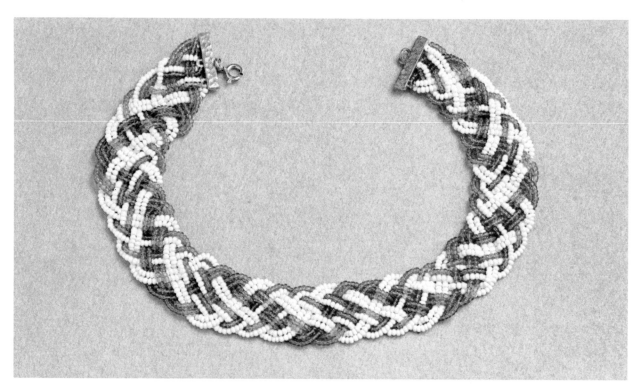

Braided Necklace of seed beads (see page 27)

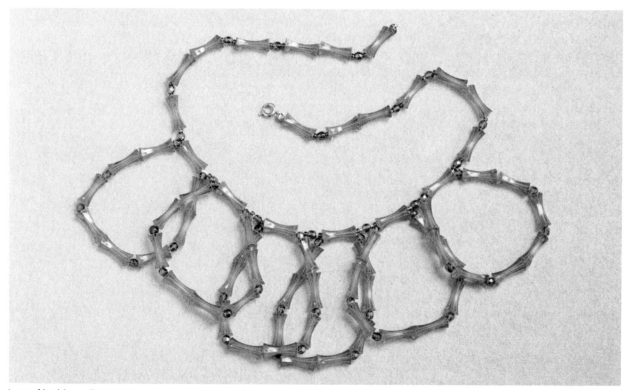

Loop Necklace (instructions on facing page)

Loop Necklace

Materials
68 ½-inch tube beads
51 4-mm round or faceted beads
30 seed beads, the same color as the 4-mm beads
4 yards beading thread (to be used double)
2 bead cups
2 jump rings
Spring ring
Beading needle
Jewelers' cement

Thread the needle and double the thread. Push the two free ends through one of the bead cups until 6 inches have come through. Knot and reknot the thread until you have a substantial lump in the bead cup, leaving an end of about 1 inch. (See page 19.)

Thread the beads in the following pattern, pushing them firmly against the bead cup: One tube, one seed, one 4-mm, one seed, two tubes, one seed, one 4-mm, one seed. Do this until you have strung a total of seven tubes, ending with one tube, one seed, one 4-mm, one seed.

Thread one tube, one 4-mm, two tubes, one 4-mm. Do that two more times. Go back through the first tube in this paragraph; pull taut to form your first loop. String one seed bead, one 4-mm, one seed bead. Repeat the loop pattern five more times, stringing between each loop a seed bead, a 4-mm, and a seed bead.

Repeat the pattern for the first seven tube beads to the end. Thread a second bead cup at the end, cut off the needle, and make another knot like that in the first bead cup.

Cover each knot with a thin layer of jewelers' cement and let dry. Cut off excess thread. Attach one jump ring to each bead cup, and, with needle-nose pliers, close the bead cup. Attach the spring ring to one of the jump rings.

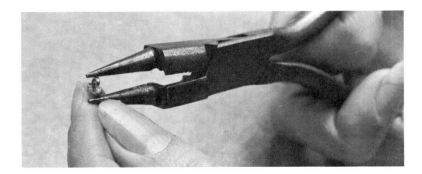

Closing bead cup

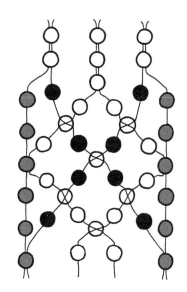

Threading for pendant

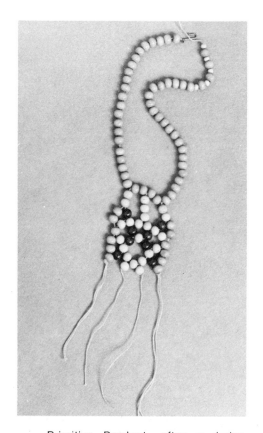

Primitive Pendant, after a design found by Joan Edwards.

Primitive Pendant

The detail of an Ecuadorian seed bead necklace diagramed here has been enlarged to make a pendant that is the focal point of a plain choker. Very often details of primitive necklaces can be enlarged in this manner to make effective, important designs.

Materials
95 8-mm round wooden beads—64 of color A, 23 of color B, 8 of color C
5 3-mm round wooden beads
1 spool pearl embroidery cotton, #5
Darning needle
Jump ring
Hook

On embroidery cotton, begin a single-strand choker of beads by alternating 3-mm round beads with beads of color A until you have strung all five 3-mm wooden beads. Complete the choker in beads of color A. Finish by adding the jump ring and hook. (See finishing instructions for Two-Needle Choker, page 33.)

At the center of the necklace, loop a yard-long strand of thread and knot between beads so there are two ½-yard ends hanging free. Cut two more yard-long pieces of thread. Knot one piece of thread two beads to the right of the center strands and the other piece of thread two beads to the left of the center strands.

Follow the diagram to make the pendant.

Finish by knotting each strand directly under the last bead, leaving 1 or 2 inches of thread hanging free.

Two-Needle Beading

You can achieve many interesting beading effects if you use two needles. Once you begin experimenting you'll find you can develop interesting shapes on your own.

Classic Eye Necklace

Materials
1 string black seed beads
1 string amber seed beads
44 3-mm round black beads
20 8-mm round amber beads
3 yards beading thread
2 beading needles

Thread two needles with 1½ yards of thread on each. Pass both needles, together, through the following beads: *Five black seed beads, five amber seed beads, two 3-mm black beads. Separate the needles and string on each: Ten amber seed beads, ten black seed beads.

String one large amber bead on one needle, then put the other needle through the same bead in the opposite direction. Pull taut. Separately, string each needle with ten black beads, then ten amber beads.

Thread the needles together through two 3-mm black beads, five amber seed beads, five black seed beads, one large amber bead, three 3-mm black beads** two large amber beads, three 3-mm black beads, one large amber bead.* Repeat pattern between the single * until the necklace is about 2 inches shorter than the desired length, ending the last repeat at double **. End by putting both needles through one large amber bead, three 3-mm black beads, one large amber bead, three 3-mm black beads, one large amber bead.

See page 19 for instructions on finishing a necklace without findings.

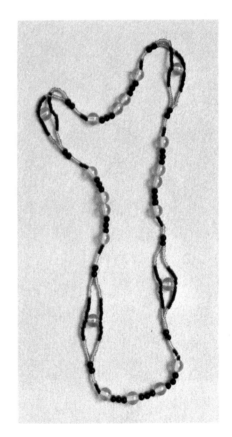

This Classic Eye Necklace is a basic example of two-needle beading: simple circles of seed beads with larger beads in the center.

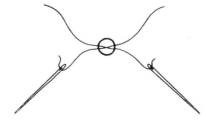

Two needles passing through bead in opposite directions

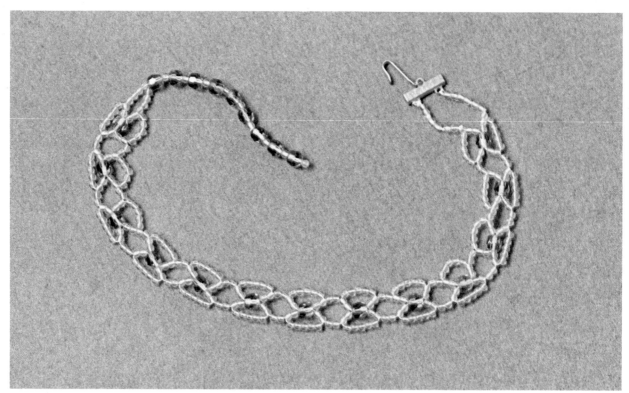

Two-Needle Choker (instructions on facing page)

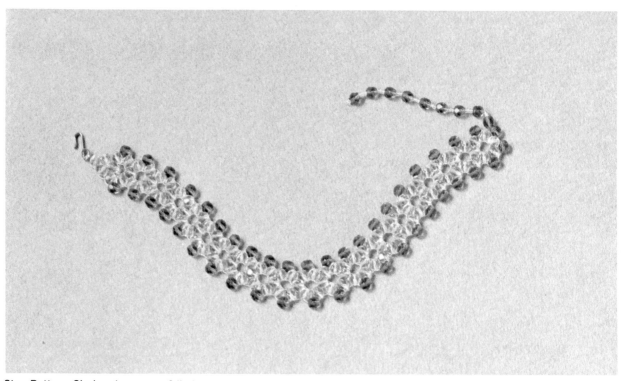

Star Pattern Choker (see page 34)

Two-Needle Choker

Materials

4 strings (100 per string) 3-mm round beads
22 6-mm crystal beads
3 yards beading thread
2 beading needles
Hook
Jump ring
2-holed necklace end
Jewelers' cement

Thread two needles with 1½ yards of thread on each. String one 3-mm bead on both needles (together) and go through again with both needles, leaving 6-inch ends. Putting both needles through, alternate crystal and 3-mm beads for about 3 inches, ending with a crystal bead.

String six 3-mm round beads and one crystal bead on one needle. String six round beads on the other needle and go through the crystal bead in the same direction as the first needle.

*On one needle, string seven 3-mm beads. With the same needle go back through the last two beads below the crystal, through the crystal and through the next two 3-mm beads to make a loop. Repeat on the other side with the other needle.

String four 3-mm round beads on each needle, add one crystal bead and go through it with both needles.* Repeat the pattern between * until the choker is of the desired length.

To finish: After you have made a set of double loops, string seven 3-mm beads on each needle. Attach the necklace end by passing a threaded needle through one hole and wrapping the thread around the hole two or three times. Go back through two beads, knot around the thread, go back through two more beads and knot again. Put a dab of jewelers' cement on the thread end close to the last knot; pull through two more beads and cut. Repeat with the other needle through the second hole in the necklace end. Attach jump ring and choker hook.

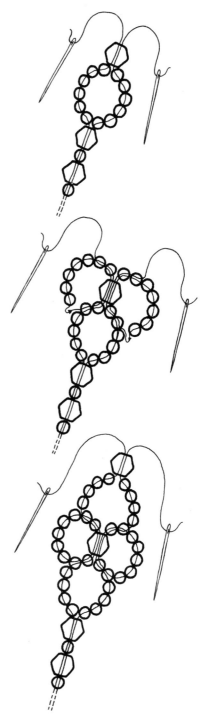

Using two needles to form pattern for choker (after a design by Lurlene Collum)

Star Pattern Choker

Materials

(These materials are enough for an 11-inch choker with a 3½-inch tail and 1 inch of findings.)

53 dark 6-mm crystal beads
109 pale 6-mm crystal beads
17 pale seed beads
3 yards beading thread
2 beading needles
Bead cup
Jump ring
Hook
Jewelers' cement

Circles will be of pale beads, edges will be of dark beads. The necklace is pictured on page 32.

First circle: Thread one needle at each end of the beading thread. String beads A and B on either needle and move them to center of thread. String bead C on one needle and pass other needle through in the opposite direction. Pass the left needle through bead D. String bead E on either needle and pass the other needle through in the opposite direction. String bead F on the left needle. String bead G on one needle and pass the other needle through in the opposite direction. String bead H with the left needle. String bead I on either needle and pass the other needle through in the opposite direction. String beads J and K on the right needle. Pass the same needle up through bead B and back down again through bead J. String bead L on either needle and pass the other needle through in the opposite direction. Then pull the work taut. This will complete the first circle.

Second circle: String bead M on the right-hand thread. String bead N on either needle and pass the other needle through in the opposite direction. String bead O on the right-hand thread. String bead P on either needle and pass the other needle through in the opposite direction. String beads Q and R on the left needle. With the same needle, go down through H and up through Q. String S on either needle, and with the other needle pass through in the opposite direction. Pull the work taut.

Third circle: Bead S is in the same position as bead E in the overall pattern, so begin the third circle as though you were stringing bead F. Continue in this manner until the choker is of the desired length.

To finish choker: Weave threads back through the pattern until both ends emerge from the last center bead. String one bead on

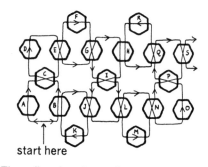

start here

Threading for star pattern

each thread and pass each thread through a third bead. Pass both threads through the bead cup and cut, leaving enough thread to make a substantial knot. Cement the knot and let dry. Close the bead cup around the jump ring which has been attached to the hook.

To make tail: String one seed bead, one dark crystal, *two light seed beads, one dark crystal bead*. Repeat between * until the tail is of the desired length. Pass a needle through bead C of the first circle, knot, weave through one bead, knot, weave through two beads and cut. Put a needle on the loose thread at other end of tail, go around first seed bead and back into tail, knotting, weaving, and cementing until end is secure.

Bamboo Necklace

Materials
26 1½-inch bamboo tubes
225 5-mm round wooden beads
10 yards beading thread
2 beading needles
Bead cup
Hook
Jump ring
Jewelers' cement

Thread one needle at each end of beading thread. String five 5-mm beads and move them to the center of the thread. Pass both ends of the thread, in opposite directions, through a sixth bead. String four more beads, two on each strand. Add a bead to either thread end and go through it in the opposite direction with the other end. Continue making loops in this manner until you have made six of them.

Add six 5-mm beads to each end of the thread. Pass both ends through a tube bead in opposite directions. *Add two 5-mm beads to the left thread and four 5-mm beads to the right thread. Pass both ends, in opposite directions, through a tube bead.* Repeat steps between * until the necklace rests comfortably around the neck.

Add six 5-mm beads to each end of thread. Pass both needles through one 5-mm bead in opposite directions. *Place one bead on each end of the thread. Pass both ends through a third bead in opposite directions.* Continue as between * until you have three small circles. Place one more 5-mm bead on each thread. Pass both ends of the thread through a bead cup, knot and cement. Attach jump ring to bead cup. Add the hook to the jump ring.

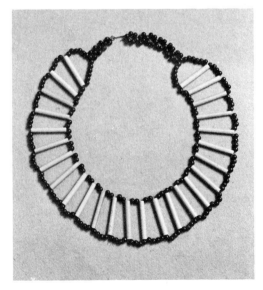

Bamboo Necklace. For detail of closing, see page 20.

Bibs

Beaded bibs and collars always look impressive, yet they are simple to work once the basic technique is understood. The directions given here are common to many types of bibs and can be used with all kinds of beads.

Basic Bib

Materials
Small package seed beads
2 packages E beads
35 8-mm beads (matte finish millefiori were used here)
10 yards beading thread
2 beading needles
2 bead cups
Jump ring
Spring ring
Jewelers' cement

Holding the two needles together, with a double thread 1½ yards long on one and a double thread 3 yards long on the other, string beads in the following pattern for 4 inches: One E bead, three seed beads, one E bead.

After 4 inches, separate the two needles. Leave the one with the longer thread free. With the other, *thread one E bead, three seed beads, one E bead, three seed beads. Go back through the first E bead from left to right, to form a loop with the E bead at the top and bottom. Using the same needle, string three seed beads, one E bead, three seed beads, one E bead, three seed beads.* Repeat between * for 6 inches.

Next, repeat the pattern of the first 4 inches. Loop thread around last bead and cut off the first needle, leaving a 6-inch end.

Pick up the second threaded needle. Pass it down three seed beads on the left side of the first loop and through the bottom E bead of the first loop. String nine E beads, one 8-mm bead, eight E beads, and go back through the same E bead in the first small loop from left to right. String three seed beads, one E bead, three seed beads, one E bead, three seed beads. Go through the bottom E bead of second small loop. String nine E beads, one 8-mm bead, four E beads. Go up through the fifth E bead at the right side of the first long loop, string four E beads and go back through the bottom E bead of the second small loop from left to right.

This Egyptian faïence collar from the eighteenth dynasty was worked by increasing the numbers of beads in each row. The Metropolitan Museum of Art, bequest of Howard Carter, 1939.

Continue making large, attached loops in this manner until you have gone through all the small loops. After you go through the E bead in the last small loop, string only eight E beads before the 8-mm bead.

When the last loop has been made, bring your needle down through the end row of E beads and the last 8-mm bead, from right to left. String four E beads, one 8-mm bead, and four E beads. Pass through the next 8-mm bead of the previous row from right to left. Continue in this manner until you have gone through the last 8-mm bead of the previous row.

String five E beads and go through the last 8-mm bead strung from left to right. String four E beads, one 8-mm bead, four E beads and go through the next 8-mm bead from left to right.

Continue the necklace in this manner until you have only one 8-mm bead left. Go back through a few E beads in the next loop to the right. Knot. Continue weaving and knotting until the thread is secure.

To finish: Knot each thread end of the necklace into a bead cup and cement. Add a spring ring to one end and a jump ring to the other.

The Basic Bib pictured here is worked by decreasing the number of loops in each row. The technique is similar to that used in Mexican Lace (see page 39). The difference in threading at the end and the beginning of the rows causes the bib to get narrower toward the bottom. The two techniques can be combined for shaped pieces.

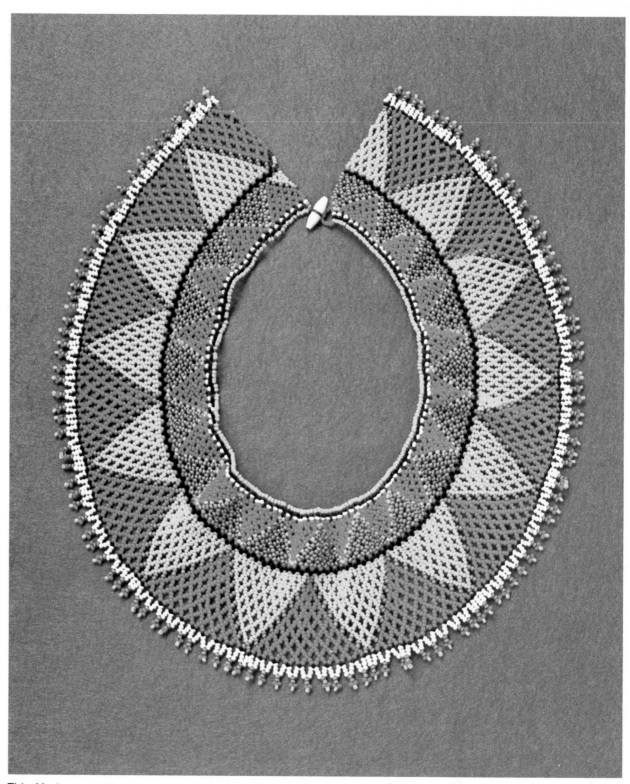

This Mexican seed bead collar uses the Mexican Lace technique and increases in every row. Owned by Eleanor Moore.

Mexican Lace

This lacy, open beadwork technique is used by Mexicans and Africans alike to create intricate, difficult-seeming patterns. Like Peyote beading (see page 52), this technique, once learned, is invaluable, and has many applications. It is also quite simple. The only slightly complicated step is at the end of a row.

Technique and Sampler

Materials

50 E beads, dark color
50 E beads, light color
5 yards monofilament or beading thread

Work with two colors of beads. Thread monofilament or beading thread with beads in the following pattern: Two dark, one light, *three dark, one light*. Repeat between * until you have fifteen beads strung, then string two dark beads to finish the first row.

Begin the second row by stringing four light beads. Then go back from right to left through the third bead from the end in the first row (the first light bead as you read the row from right to left). Pull tight. String three light beads and, going from right to left, go through the next light bead in the first row. Pull tight. Continue working across the row in this manner, stringing three light beads and going back through every fourth bead in the first row, until you reach the last light bead at the left end of the first row. Go through this bead and the two next to it (the first two beads strung on the first row). Add four light beads and go through the two beads at the left end of the first row, from right to left. Come back down through three of the four beads just added.

Add three dark beads. Working from left to right, go through the bottom center bead of the nearest loop in the previous row. Continue working between * until you have gone through the last center bead at the right-hand end of the row. Add four light beads and go back through the center bead of the first loop of the previous row, now working from right to left.

Once you are comfortable with the technique, use this sampler to experiment with colors and patterns.

This Tshomane adornment combines Mexican Lace with long beaded strands and buttons. Lowie Museum of Anthropology, University of California, Berkeley.

start
here

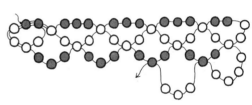

Threading for Mexican Lace

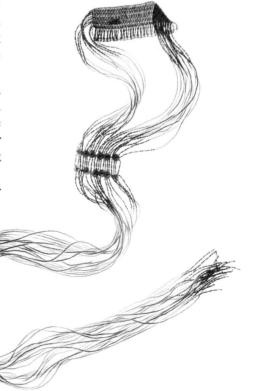

Mexican Lace Window Hanging

The 8-mm round beads used for this window hanging make clear the honeycomb structure of Mexican Lace beadwork.

Materials

500 (approximately) 8-mm round transparent glass or plastic beads, 60 of them in a dark color

15 yards monofilament for project, extra for hanging

12-inch dowel

Jewelers' cement

Cut a 4-yard length of monofilament and make a large, sturdy knot at one end. String beads in the pattern shown for section A. Repeat, making a second section A. Cut a 4-yard length of monofilament. Knot as for section A. Work pattern as shown for section B.

To attach hanging to dowel, run a 15-inch length of monofilament through the top beads of each section. Position sections under dowel and drill six holes so sections can be attached as shown. Pass strands through holes and knot, leaving ends free. Drill another hole in center of dowel for hanging entire piece.

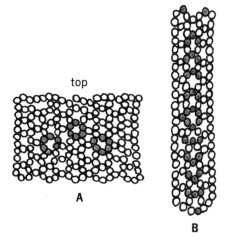

top

top

A

B

Work patterns as above. To hang, see photo. (Note that both A pieces are hung sideways. The B piece is hung as it is worked.)

Mexican Lace Window Hanging, with dowel. Although this particular piece was worked in two colors of 8-mm glass beads, patterns can be developed in many colors, and any kind of bead can be used.

Wire and Beads

Working with wire and beads is simple. You can make rings, bracelets, chokers, free-form sculpture, doll-house furniture, ponytail rings, napkin holders, baskets, and flowers. A few ideas are offered here. Once you start experimenting, you'll discover how to make many other interesting wire shapes.

Beaded Ring

Materials
12 (approximately) bugle beads
1 yard 28-gauge beading wire

Using a wire cutter or a pair of needle-nose pliers, cut off about 1 yard of wire. String one bugle bead and slide it to the middle of the wire. String a second bugle, pass the other end of the wire through it in the opposite direction, and pull taut. The first two bugle beads should now be lying next to each other. Keep stringing bugle beads in this manner until the ring is long enough to fit around your finger.

Join by passing the two ends of the wire back through the first bead. Pass the two ends of the wire through the next three or four beads, then clip the ends.

You can make rings with rows of seed beads simply by treating each row as though it were an individual bead. Make sure the beads in the first few rows you string have holes large enough for four thicknesses of wire to pass through.

Wire Choker

Materials
200 (approximately) 5-mm round wooden beads, 100 in each of two
   colors
4 yards 28-gauge beading wire

String one bead of color A (see diagram) on the wire and move it to the center. Holding the two ends of the wire together, thread beads on both wires for about 2½ inches.

Separate wires and thread one bead of color A on each. String two beads of color B on one of the wires, then go through both beads with the other wire in the opposite direction. *String two beads of color A on each wire. String two beads of color A on one wire and pass the other wire through in the opposite direction*, making a loop of eight beads.

Continue as between *, alternating loops of color A and

Assortment of beaded rings, all worked on 28-gauge beading wire

Beginning of Wire Choker

Wire Choker (see page 41)

color B until the choker is 1½ inches shorter than the desired length. Add two beads on either wire and pass the other wire through in the opposite direction. Add two beads of one color to one wire and two beads of the same color to the other wire. Add one bead of the other color to either wire and go back through the last three beads added in the opposite direction with the other wire. Repeat for the other side of the loop. Work ends of the wire back through the work as for finishing rings (see page 41). Clip wire.

Choker closes by hooking the first beads strung through the last loop made.

Wire Bracelet

Materials
17 ½-inch wooden tube beads
12 8-mm round wooden beads
15 5-mm round wooden beads
2 yards 28-gauge beading wire

Begin as for the wire choker (see page 41), using 5-mm round beads. When you have threaded seven beads, separate the wires and string three 5-mm beads on each wire. Pass both ends of the wire through one tube bead, going in opposite directions. Pull taut. String one tube bead on each wire. Pass both wires, going in the same direction, through an 8-mm round bead. Separate the wires and string a tube bead on each of them. Pass both ends of wire, in opposite directions, through a third tube bead.

String two 8-mm beads on each wire. String another 8-mm bead on either wire and pass the other wire through in the opposite direction. String one tube bead on each wire. String a tube bead on either wire and pass the other wire through in the opposite direction. String one tube bead on each wire. String an 8-mm bead on either wire and pass the other wire through in the opposite direction. String two 8-mm beads on each wire.

String a tube bead on either wire and pass the other wire through in the opposite direction. String one tube bead on each wire. Pass both wires, in the same direction, through an 8-mm bead. String one tube bead on each wire. Pass both wires, in opposite directions, through a tube bead.

String three 5-mm beads on each wire. Pass one wire back through three 5-mm beads in the opposite direction. Repeat with the other wire. Work each wire back through the work for a few beads, then clip the ends. As in the wire choker, the first end made forms a hook that goes through the last loop to close the bracelet.

This Wire Bracelet and the choker pictured above use the self-closing tail and loop method (see pages 20 and 21 for other closures).

Bead Looms

Bead looms are almost always identified with American Indian beadwork. They were extensively used by American Indians in every part of the country and were the source of many extraordinary pieces. Spectacular loom work was done by the Ojibwa, Navajo, Sioux, Ute, Blackfoot, Apache, and Cheyenne. It is still done by many of these tribes today.

A bead loom is simple to work with and simple to build. Inexpensive looms like the small one pictured on page 13 are available, but their major drawback is their shortness. In order to make anything longer than 4 or 5 inches you must continually loosen, unroll, then reroll your work. This is distracting, and can cause uneven tension in the finished piece. However, you can construct a basic loom of your own, using easily obtainable materials and only a few tools, that will permit continuous working on much larger pieces. Directions for making this loom are given on the following pages. The process will probably take no more than two hours, excluding drying time for the glue.

This is not an adjustable loom, and your finished piece will be no longer than the distance between the end bolts used to separate the warp threads and no wider than the length of these bolts.

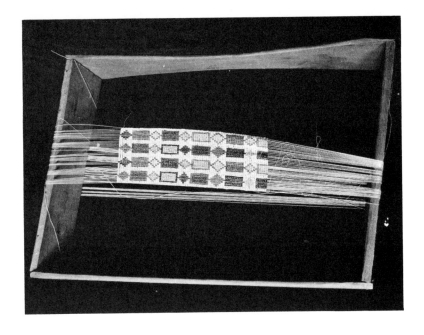

Square frame bead loom, used by the Menominee Indians. Courtesy of the American Museum of Natural History.

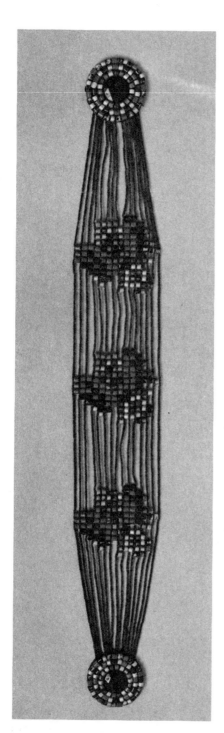

1940s loomed piece with sections of warp left unbeaded. Owned by Eleanor Moore.

Making a Loom

Materials

1 piece of wood, ¾ × 3 × 36 inches (try to use solid wood, such as pine or poplar, rather than plywood)
4 pieces of wood, each ¾ × 1½ × 4 inches
2 bolts, ¼ × 5 or 6 inches
2 nuts to fit bolts
Wood glue
8 1½-inch finish nails
2 1-inch or 1½-inch common nails

Tools

Hammer
Saw (or get wood cut to size at lumberyard)
Drill with ¼-inch bit plus a bit that is thinner than the finish nails
Pliers
Ruler
Pencil

Substitutions: You may change the length and width of piece A (see diagram) to suit your own needs, but remember to change the length of the bolts if you widen piece A. You can also buy threaded steel rod in almost any length to substitute for the bolts if you want a very wide loom. If you do this, you will need four nuts since the threaded rod will not have a head like the bolts.

Construction

Drill a ¼-inch hole through each B piece approximately ½ inch from the top. Be sure to center each hole so that it will align properly with the hole in the opposite B piece.

Hammer two finish nails into each B piece as shown in the diagram. The nails should be ⅜ inch from the bottom. Do not drive the nails in all the way—only until their points appear in the back of the wood. To prevent the wood from splitting, it's a good idea to drill holes in the B pieces for the finish nails. Be sure to use a bit that is smaller than the nails.

Measure about 2 inches from each end of piece A on both sides and draw a straight line parallel to the edge at each end. Glue the B pieces to the A piece as shown, positioning the B pieces by placing them against the lines drawn on piece A. Keep the B pieces straight and flush along the bottom. Now drive the finish nails all the way through the B pieces and into piece A. Let the glue dry for at least 24 hours.

Hammer one common nail into each end of piece A. Be sure to leave ¼ inch of the nail exposed.

Push the bolts through the holes in the B pieces so that each forms a "bridge" across the loom. Attach the nuts. Be sure not to tighten the nuts too far as that will place great strain on the bond between the B pieces and piece A. The nuts are to prevent the bolts from slipping out.

General instructions

Unless otherwise specified, the instructions that follow are given for working with seed beads. However, you can make unique loomed items using any size beads. Adapt your loom for larger beads by using heavier thread for both warp and weft, and by placing warp threads as far apart as necessary.

Because seed beads are wider than they are high, using ordinary graph paper to indicate loomed designs will give a distorted picture of the finished pattern. Special beading paper has been used for the patterns given in this book and is available through Walbead (see page 64).

Finished Bead Loom

Construction diagram

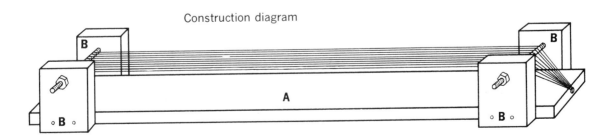

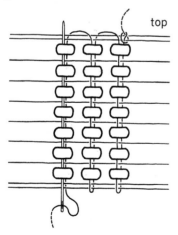

(Below) Work the bead loom from right to left, following pattern diagram. Push the beads up between the warp threads with your forefinger. (Below right) Pattern for pink and blue Loomed Belt. Read the pattern for each row from the top down, working from right to left.

Loomed Belt

Materials
1 bunch pale blue transparent seed beads
2 strings pale pink transparent seed beads
1 spool beading thread
Beading needle
Belt buckle
½-inch-wide strip grosgrain ribbon
Jewelers' cement

Thread loom by knotting one end of the thread around nail A. Run the thread through the first space between threads or coils of bolt B and on through the first space between coils at the opposite end of the loom (bolt C). Loop thread around nail D and bring it back through the first space between the coils on the bolts on both ends of the loom (C, B). Your first warp thread is now doubled. Wrap thread around nail A. Place thread between the next two coils and then through corresponding coils at the opposite end of the loom. Loop the thread around nail D and place it between the next two coils. Continue in this way until you have eight warp threads, seven spaces. (When threading a bead loom you will always have one more thread than the number of beads across.) Double the last warp thread in the same way you doubled the first. The end threads are doubled to provide added strength. Attach the thread to the nail by looping it around the nail a couple of times, then knotting and cutting it.

Wax a comfortable length of thread and thread your needle. Knot the weaving thread around the warp thread farthest from you, leaving an end of about 6 inches.

String one row of beads according to the pattern, working each pattern row from the top down. In other words, the first bead you put on the needle should be the bead farthest from you in the pattern. Push the beads down on your weaving thread, hold the thread with the beads under the warp threads, and, with your finger, push the beads up so that one bead is between each two warp threads. Making sure your needle is above your warp threads, push it through your row of beads again, starting with the bead closest to you. Continue in this way.

top

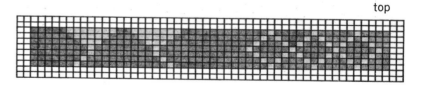

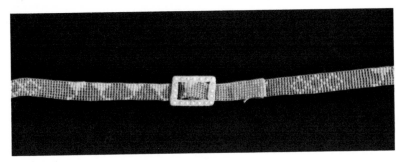

The Loomed Belt at the left (see pattern, page 46) and the two belts below are finished with conventional buckles. One end of the belt is cemented to (or sewn around) the center shank of the buckle. The other end is pulled through the buckle and holds by friction.

Seed beads vary slightly in size. To keep your work neat and even, try to select beads of uniform size. As you experiment with loom work you will be able to do this easily.

When your weaving thread becomes too short to work with, knot it around the warp thread farthest from you, then push it back through the beads in the row just before the last row worked, knot it around itself in the middle of the row, pull it through the rest of the beads in the row, pull taut and cut. Begin a new thread by pulling it through the last row worked, leaving a tail to hold onto as you knot it around the far warp threads twice. Cut the tail and you're ready to start beading again.

Continue until the belt is of the desired length, remembering to leave an extra inch for the end that gets wrapped around the buckle.

To finish: There are several ways to finish off loomed work (see page 20). For most items, I suggest weaving the end of your weaving thread back and forth through the warp threads until you have a selvage of about half an inch. Run jewelers' cement over this selvage while it's still on the loom. Do the same at the other end of the belt, using the tail of thread left at the beginning. Let the cement dry overnight, then cut the work from the loom.

If the belt buckle you have chosen is narrow enough from the center shaft to the inside of the outer edge, you can use a buckle without a tongue. Friction will hold the belt closed.

If this is the case, wrap one end of the belt around the center of the buckle and cement. Cement a piece of grosgrain ribbon to the selvage at the other end and fold back so ribbon cements selvage against the end of the belt.

If you wish, you can buy buckles with tongues to go through holes. These can be used with strips of leather made to attach to the buckle and strips of leather prepunched with holes to attach to the other end of the belt. If you make a belt for this kind of buckle, don't forget to take into account the length of the leather pieces and make your beaded belt correspondingly shorter.

To join ends of a loomed piece, weave a thread back and forth between the beads from top to bottom, then weave again from bottom to top. This may be done a second time for further reinforcement.

To conceal selvage of a loomed piece, wrap a length of grosgrain ribbon around it and cement the ends of the grosgrain in place.

Bracelets and Headbands

To make a bracelet, headband, or ponytail holder, use round elastic for warp threads and beading thread for weaving (or weft) thread. Do not put any tension on the elastic when you thread the loom. End threads should not be doubled. Work the same way as for a loomed belt (page 46).

To finish: Make selvage at each end in the same way as suggested for the loomed belt. Cement and let dry on loom. Cut the piece off the loom and sew the ends together by sewing back and forth through the end rows of the beads, as shown in the diagram. Turn the bracelet inside out and cement a short piece of grosgrain ribbon (pink the edges to keep them from unraveling) around the selvage, making sure you cover all thread ends. Let dry.

The Random, Star, and Lightning Flash designs pictured here are just three examples of the many pattern possibilities in loomed work.

Loomed Choker

Materials

5 large blue glass Israeli beads
12 yards dark green rattail
12 yards silver rattail, divided into two 6-yard sections
Beading needle
½-inch wide strip of silver satin ribbon
Jewelers' cement

Thread your loom with green rattail, placing the warp threads between every third coil until you have ten warp threads. Do not double the end threads. Take one 6-yard length of silver rattail and start weaving about 8 inches from one end of the loom. Weave through the warp threads in a simple "over one thread, under one thread" pattern. Make sure you don't pull weft threads too tightly or your choker will be pulled out of shape. When 5 inches are woven, begin the center section, which will measure 2 inches. Leave five long loops facing you, spacing them one row apart. Attach the other length of silver rattail here, making the end of the old thread and the end of the new thread two parts of one loop, as the loops will be cut anyway.

After completing the center section, continue as from the beginning until the choker measures 12 inches. Cut the choker from the loom. At one end of the choker, separate the warp threads into two bunches of five threads each and make "buttons" by knotting each bunch. Divide the warp threads at the other end into two bunches of five threads each and braid each bunch separately for the two loops.

Cut two equal lengths of ribbon so that, when the edges are folded under, each equals the width of the choker. With ends folded under, sew each ribbon to the back of the choker, catching the loop ends and any loose weft thread ends under each one.

Place one bead on each loop and make a double knot underneath. Cement the knots and cut the loose ends.

Detail of closure for Loomed Choker

This Loomed Choker illustrates one of the ways a bead loom can combine fiber and beads. Open spaces can be left between beads; different weaving patterns can be used.

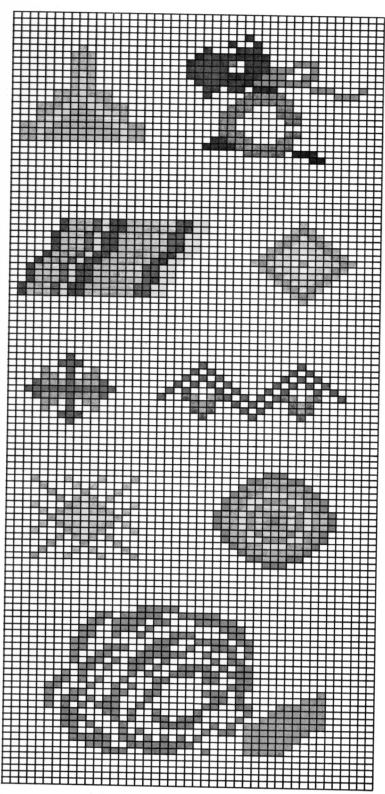

A few pattern possibilities for loomed work

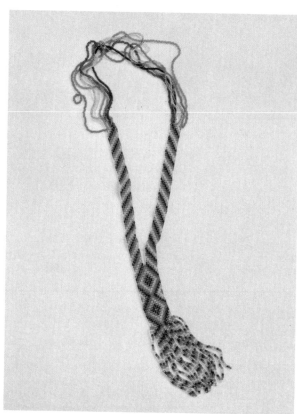

Indian Loomed Necklace With Fringe (instructions on facing page; patterns below)

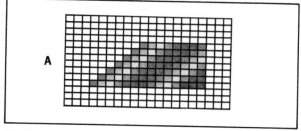

A

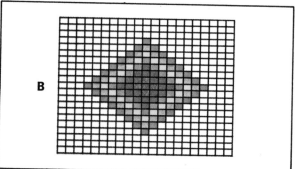

B

Threading for patterns A and B

Indian Loomed Necklace With Fringe

Materials

3 strings seed beads in each of following colors: red, orange,
  yellow, green, blue, indigo, violet
1 spool nylon beading thread
4 beading needles
Jewelers' cement

Thread the loom with sixteen rows of thread (fifteen spaces).
Starting 10 inches from the right end of the loom, work pattern A as shown on page 50 for 8 inches, using only the top seven spaces. Leaving the center space empty, work pattern A in the bottom seven spaces until the bottom half equals 8 inches also.

Using all fifteen spaces, work pattern B for two repeats.

Cut the bottom thread from the loom, attach a needle, and, continuing in the rainbow pattern, string eight repeats. Loop the thread around the last bead strung and go back through two or three beads. Make sure the fringe is pulled snugly back against the body of the necklace, knot the thread, cement, go back through two or more beads, pull taut, and cut the thread. Repeat this procedure for each remaining thread.

Cut the other end of the necklace from the loom, as close to the roller as possible. Put a needle on the top thread and string with red beads, leaving enough free thread to make a knotted closing. Repeat this procedure with the bottom thread. Join the two beaded strands. Repeat this procedure with orange beads and the next two inner strands, one at the top and one at the bottom. Make this loop a little smaller than the first. Continue in this manner until all the ends have been closed.

Bead Weaving Without a Loom

In this method of weaving beads, the beads lie like bricks, one diagonally above another. The texture is firm, and many items can be made this way: trivets, place mats, coasters, wall hangings. Special "tile-craft" graph paper is sold by Walbead (see page 64) for designing patterns to use with this method.

Techniques

There are two methods for weaving without a loom. For items with an even number of rows, you weave with only one thread; for articles with an odd number of rows, you weave with two threads.

Even Row (One-Needle) Technique

This method is also called Peyote beading (or twill beading) and was used by the ancient Egyptians and by American Indians of the Southwest. Items made by this method were used in peyote ceremonies. It's a versatile, simple, and relaxing beadwork method, creating an attractive, solid texture. It can be done around a core of rope to make a spiral pattern. Any beads of uniform size are appropriate for this technique. However, be sure that the beads used are large enough for the thread to pass through twice.

Technique and Sampler

Materials

1 string seed beads, color A
1 string seed beads, color B
2 yards beading thread
Beading needle

For your first Peyote sampler, use two colors of seed beads. Thread your needle with the appropriate thread in a manageable length, and make a large knot about 2 inches from the end of thread. String one bead of color A and slide it down to the knot. String eleven more beads of color A.

Using color B, string a thirteenth bead and go back through the third bead from the needle (the eleventh bead strung). Pull tight. String another bead of color B and go back through the ninth bead of the first row. Pull tight. Keep adding beads of color B and going back through each bead in the first row, pulling tightly after each addition. Continue in this way, work-

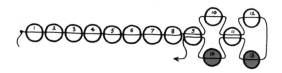

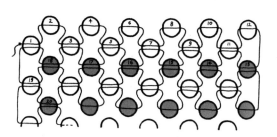

Threading for Peyote beading (bead weaving without a loom, Even Row Technique)

ing from right to left, until you have gone through all the beads in the first row.

Using color A, add a bead. Working now from left to right, go through the first bead of color B in previous row. Pull tight. Add another bead in color A and go through the next bead in color B. Continue in this manner.

Don't be alarmed if the first couple of rows look sloppy. Your work will smooth out as you continue beading. As with loomed work, beads should be selected so that they are of equal size. Note that you cannot get an odd number of rows when you do Peyote beading.

As you work you will see that each new bead nestles into the space left between the two beads in the previous row. When you alternate horizontal rows of two colors, Peyote beading forms a pattern of vertical rows of each color. Try experimenting to see what happens when you use three, four, or even more colors.

This tile bead coaster was made using the Even Row Technique.

Peyote Belt

Materials
1000 each of dark brown and tan 5-mm round wooden beads
150 natural 5-mm round wooden beads
65 each of red and orange 5-mm round wooden beads
1 spool dark brown Knit-Cro-Sheen
Yarn needle
Buckle
Jewelers' cement

This random belt was made with a first row of twelve beads. If you plan to use a buckle, work a sampler first (see page 52) to make sure the buckle you have chosen will accommodate that number of beads. If not, change your pattern accordingly, or use a loop and button or tie closure. (See page 21 for instructions on making this kind of closing.)

Before you end off an old thread that has become too short, begin a new thread by putting the needle through the bead three rows above the last bead added. Leave a 3-inch tail. Knot. Weave through three beads, knot, weave through three more beads, and come out through the appropriate bead in a position to work. Cut tail of new thread, *then* end off old thread. If you use this method, there will be no chance of losing your place, even in your first Peyote work.

To end off the thread, weave back and forth through one row for three beads, knot around a connecting thread, work back through three more beads, and knot again. Weave through three more beads, pull taut, and cut.

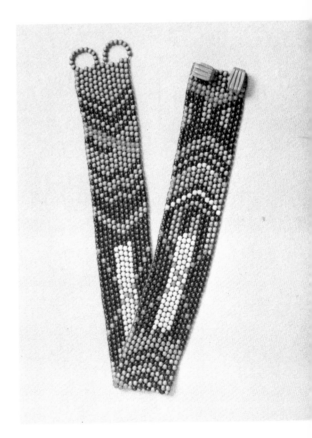

Peyote Belt. Peyote beading requires no equipment, and can be done anywhere, like needlepoint.

Wire bracelet woven in Odd Row Technique, made off the loom.

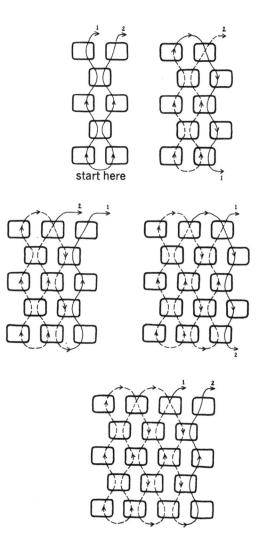

start here

Threading for bead weaving without a loom, Odd Row Technique.

Odd Row (Two-Needle) Technique

Place a needle on each end of the thread. String two beads on one needle and move them down to the center of the thread. Pass both needles, in the same direction, through a third bead. Then string one bead on each needle. Pass both needles, in the same direction, through a sixth bead. Continue in this manner until the piece is the desired length, ending the first row with the addition of two beads. Bring the left-hand thread (thread 1) down through a right-hand bead. Pass thread 1 down through a new bead, then through the right-hand bead just below. Continue in this manner until thread 1 emerges from the bottom of the work. Pass thread 1 through a new bead, then up through the right-hand bead directly above. Continue in this manner until thread 1 emerges from the top bead (newly added).

Thread 1 and thread 2 are now side by side at the top of the work. Thread 2 is to the left of thread 1. Pass thread 2 down through the bead just added and continue as for the first downward row of thread 1, until thread 2 emerges from the bottom of the work. Continue upward as for thread 1, until thread 2 emerges from the top of the work. Thread 1 is now to the left of thread 2 and is in position to cross to the right and begin working down again.

Finish as for Even Row Technique (page 52).

Bead Embroidery

The possibilities for bead embroidery are endlessly fascinating, as is its varied history. Beads have decorated textiles since prehistoric times, and there are many ways beads and textiles can be used in combination today. Beads can be sewn in rows to make a dense covering that completely obscures the fabric underneath. (A great deal of American Indian beading was done this way, using the so-called lazy stitch.) Beads can be sewn down individually to add spots of glitter or color to an otherwise plain piece of clothing. They can be used to paint scenes, abstract patterns, or people. You can create flowing curves that are difficult to achieve with other beading methods.

Techniques

Two techniques are used most often in bead embroidery. One, using a single needle, employs the lazy stitch, in which small numbers of beads are sewn to the fabric with each stitch (the number of beads is usually eight, sewn in back and forth rows that cover the entire surface of the item being beaded). The other method uses a second needle and thread to sew long strings of beads to the fabric.

One-Needle Method

Use as strong and heavy a thread as the beads and material will allow. Place the fabric in an embroidery hoop or frame. Knot the end of your thread and pass the needle up from the bottom of the fabric. String three beads and push them close to the fabric. Bring your needle back down through the fabric as close to the last bead as possible. Bring your needle up again, keeping it as close to the last bead as you can. Put three more beads on the needle and repeat the procedure. I find bead embroidery simplified somewhat by making a backstitch through the last bead every time I bring the needle down through the fabric. This gives the beading extra strength and eliminates the difficulty of bringing the thread up through the fabric close enough to the bead so it won't be seen.

End off by bringing your thread down through the cloth, going through the last beads sewn in the opposite direction (ex-

This beaded vest, done by Crow Indians, shows how the lazy stitch can be used to create pictures. Courtesy of the American Museum of Natural History.

African textile, beaded along the edges as well as in the center. Buffalo Museum of Science.

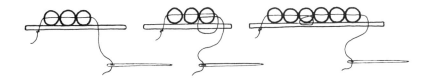

Bead embroidery using one needle, making backstitch every three beads.

cepting the end bead), going down through the cloth again, and going back through the next few beads. Keep moving back this way until you have double-stitched through a half dozen beads. Knot on the underside of the cloth and clip the thread.

Two-Needle Method

For the other bead embroidery technique, thread a needle, knot the thread, and pass the needle up from the underside of the cloth. Fill the thread with beads and lay it on the cloth. Thread another needle, knot that thread, and bring it up through the cloth after the fifth bead, passing it over the first beading thread with a tiny stitch and bringing it back down through the cloth as close to the beadwork as possible. Do this every five beads. To finish, bring the beaded needle back down through the cloth and knot. Bring the second needle down through the cloth between the next-to-last bead and the last bead, and knot.

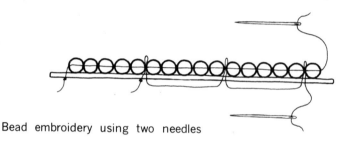

Bead embroidery using two needles

Patterns

The number of beads that you embroider with each stitch depends on the nature of your pattern. If you are working with straight lines you may be able to leave as many as eight beads with each stitch. It is easier to control the beads, of course, if you leave fewer beads with each stitch.

You can draw your design directly on the material. But if you're nervous about that, try a technique used to transfer quilting patterns: Draw the design on paper, then pierce the design with a needle, making holes about ¼ inch apart. Place the paper design on the material and dust the paper with cinnamon powder. Rub lightly. Lift the paper carefully and follow the cinnamon pattern now on your material. Any excess can be dusted off easily, and the smell is lovely.

Yoruba beaded royal crown, Nigeria. Late nineteenth century. Courtesy of the Brooklyn Museum, Carll H. De Silver Fund.

Macramé, Knitting, and Crochet

Knitting, crocheting, and macramé are crafts that combine well with beads. Here beads and the medium by which they are connected have equal weight. Attractive yarn and string textures add to the visual and tactile elements of beading, and lend themselves to rich and fruitful experimentation.

Embellish plain knit or crocheted garments by scattering beads over their surface. Knit or crochet them in as you work (see pages 59 and 61) or treat the finished garment as you would any other piece of cloth and embroider beads on to it. Macramé can be done on fine thread with small beads to create delicate objects or on heavy cord with large beads to create bolder ones.

Macramé Wind Chimes

Materials

42 4-inch brown wooden tube beads
24 1¼-inch brown wooden tube beads
33 ½-inch natural bamboo beads
96 ¼-inch black beads
Small wooden ring
6-ply natural linen cord: 14 pieces 4 yards long; 2 pieces 6 yards
  long
4¾-inch rya needle

Pass the 4-yard cords through the wooden ring, arranging them so they lie in a row over the ring and the ends are even. Pass the 6-yard cords through the ring so the shorter cords are between them. Even the ends of these longer cords, which will be referred to as the primary cords.

Use the four primary cords in pairs to tie a 3½-inch column of half square knots around the rest of the cords. Using the rya needle, thread the primary cords in opposite directions through one 4-inch tube bead. Position bead horizontally about 6½ inches below end of the half square knot column.

Divide the remaining cords into four groups so there are six cords each in two of the groups and eight cords in each of the remaining groups. With one group of six cords, tie six clove hitches (double half hitches) onto the right end of the bead. Turn the piece halfway around so that the knots are on the

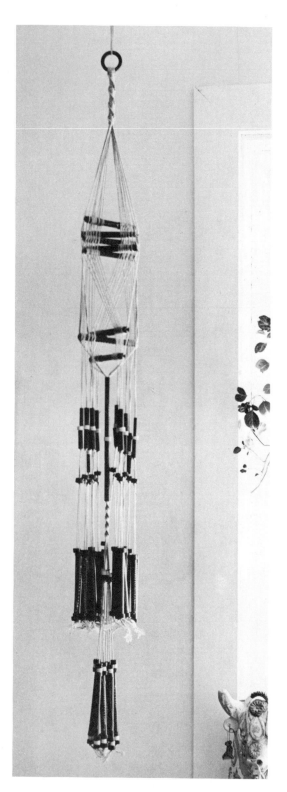

Bells for Mr. Eneos. Macramé Wind Chimes by Anita Sanders.

left side of the bead. Use the remaining group of six cords to tie six clove hitches onto the right side of the same bead.

Select a pair of cords from each group of eight cords to be the secondary cords. Thread the secondary cords in opposite directions through a 4-inch tube bead. Position this bead horizontally just below the first bead and at right angles to it. With remaining cords tie clove hitches onto either end of this bead as for first bead. Repeat knotting procedure until there are five beads positioned one below the other. The beads strung on primary cords alternate at right angles with beads strung on secondary cords.

Thread a sixth bead on secondary cords and position 5 inches below last bead. Cross the two groups of cords before tying clove hitches onto the ends of this bead. Adjust the tension on the cords so that each is taut.

Thread, position, and knot the next two beads as in the first group, except that these beads should be spaced at ½ inch to 1 inch intervals.

Bring primary and secondary cords to the center. String a 4-inch tube bead, a bamboo bead, and another 4-inch tube bead on these eight cords. With the primary cords tie a 2½-inch column of half square knots around the remaining cords in this group. Divide these eight cords into four parts. Cut the ends to make them even. Thread each pair of cords through a bamboo bead and a black bead. Position these beads 3 inches below the end of the center column of half square knots by tying overhand knots with each pair of cords.

Divide each pair of cords below last beads added and thread each individual cord as follows: black bead, bamboo bead, black bead, 4-inch tube, black bead, bamboo bead, black bead. Tie an overhand knot below last black bead, 11 inches from first overhand knot.

Divide the cords remaining in the outer groups into pairs. Thread each pair of cords as follows: 1¼-inch tube, bamboo bead, 1¼-inch tube. Tie overhand knot to position beads so that outer bamboo beads are about ¼ inch above bamboo bead in center column. String a black bead on each pair of cords and position with an overhand knot tied 2 inches below the last overhand knot.

Separate each pair of cords and thread each individual cord as follows: black bead, 4-inch tube bead, black bead. Tie overhand knot to position beads so that the center of the 4-inch tube bead is level with the bamboo and black bead combination in the center column.

To finish: Cut the ends of all cords 2 inches below final overhand knot. Unravel plies for fringe effect.

Knitting Technique

Slip the beads on the yarn or cotton.

To knit with a bead, hold it against the back of the needle, make the stitch, and pull the bead through.

To purl with a bead, push it against the front of the needle and purl as usual.

To place a bead in the hole made by a yarn over, push the bead against the front of the needle. Yarn over as usual with bead in front of needle.

Knit Purse

Materials
200 5-mm gold or silver round beads with large holes
Any soft, slightly stretchy yarn that will give the following gauge, unblocked: six stitches equal 1 inch
2 knitting needles, #2

You can make this bag any size you wish. The one shown on page 60 is 5 × 7 inches.

Pattern (even number of stitches): Knit one, *yarn over, purl two together*, knit one. Repeat this row for basic pattern stitch.

Directions: String beads on the chainette, remembering to add more beads if you are going to make a larger bag. Cast on thirty-four stitches. Work four rows in pattern. *Fifth row:* Work one bead into eighteenth stitch. (Note: this is yarn over stitch. See above for instructions on how to work beads into yarn over stitches. Almost all beads in this purse are worked into yarn over stitches.) *Row six and all even rows:* Work pattern stitch without any beads. *Row seven:* Work one bead into sixteenth and twentieth stitches. *Row nine:* Leave bead at stitches fourteen and twenty-two. *Row eleven:* Bead at twelve and twenty-four. *Row thirteen:* Bead at ten, eighteen, twenty-six. *Row fifteen:* Bead at eight, sixteen, twenty, twenty-eight. *Row seventeen:* Bead at six, fourteen, twenty-two, thirty. *Row nineteen:* Bead at four, twelve, twenty-four, thirty-two. *Row twenty-one:* Bead at two, ten, eighteen, twenty-six, thirty-four (work bead in last knit stitch; instructions are given above). *Row twenty-three:* Bead at eight, sixteen, twenty, twenty-eight. *Row twenty-five:* Bead at six, fourteen, twenty-two, thirty. *Row twenty-seven:* Bead at eighteen. *Row twenty-nine:* Bead at six, fourteen, eighteen, twenty-two, thirty. *Row thirty-one:* Bead at eighteen. *Row thirty-three:* Bead at six, fourteen, eighteen, twenty-two, thirty. *Row thirty-five:* Bead at eighteen. *Row thirty-seven:* Bead at six, fourteen, eighteen, twenty-two, thirty.

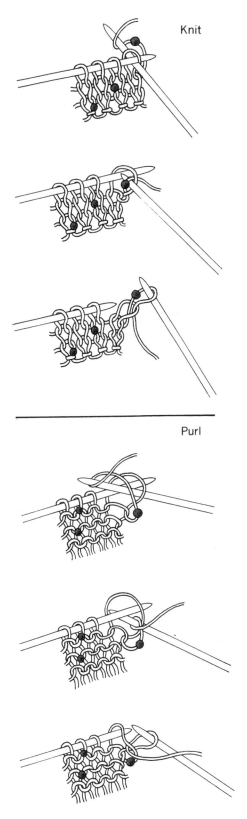

Knit

Purl

Knit Purse with beads (see page 59)

Row thirty-nine: Bead at eighteen. *Row forty-one:* Bead at six, fourteen, eighteen, twenty-two, thirty. *Row forty-three:* Bead at eighteen. *Row forty-five:* Bead at six, fourteen, eighteen, twenty-two, thirty. *Row forty-seven:* Bead at eighteen. *Row forty-nine:* Bead at fourteen, eighteen, twenty-two. *Row fifty-one and every odd row until piece measures 6½ inches:* Bead at eighteen. Work for 1 inch in pattern stitch without any beads. Then begin beading again with row where last bead was left and work back to row one to complete second side of bag.

To finish: Turn bag inside out, fold at the center, and weave together along the sides. Turn the bag right side out and pass a crocheted strand of chainette, silk, or velvet ribbon through the holes in the top row. Make large knots or add decorative ends to keep the strand from slipping back through the holes. Pull the bag closed.

Crocheted Necklace (crocheting instructions on the facing page).

Crocheting With Beads

String beads on yarn. To crochet from the front, see "Single crochet" diagram, below. To work from the back, push bead against the hook and make stitch as usual. The bead will be caught in the front of the work.

Once you've mastered this technique, you can make necklaces like the brightly colored one on the facing page. It is done all in single crochet, except for the attaching bars, which are chains and slip stitches. The oval shapes are made in this way: Double chain the first row. Single crochet back along that double chain. Single crochet twice in the last stitch and single crochet back along the underside of the double chain. Single crochet twice in the last stitch and continue back along the top. Keep going around in this way, crocheting twice in the end stitch of one side and twice in the first stitch of the opposite side.

The ovals are attached to each other by slip-stitching the bottom of one oval to the points of the oval below it.

Chain crochet

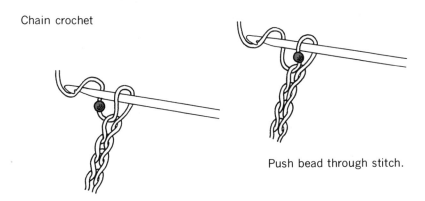

Push bead through stitch.

To begin, hold bead behind hook.

Single crochet

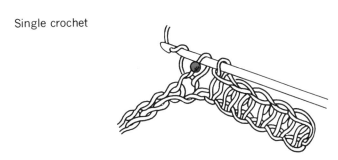

To begin, hold bead behind hook. Pull yarn through one loop, push bead through stitch, and flip bead over hook as shown. Pull through two loops.

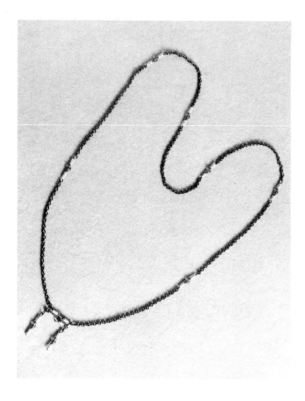

Beads and Chain

Another method of working with beads is to combine beads and chain. With beads, chain, and some findings you can create necklaces, bracelets, earrings, belts, and body jewelry. Results look professional and you need only one tool—a combined needle-nose pliers and wire cutter.

Simple Bead and Chain Necklace

Materials
10 3-mm glass beads
20 seed beads, color A
80 seed beads, color B
28 inches of chain
8 1½-inch eye pins
2 1½-inch head pins
4 jump rings
Needle-nose pliers

Using the wire cutting part of the needle-nose pliers, cut the chain into seven sections, each 4 inches long. Place on one eye pin four seed beads of color B, one seed bead of color A, one 3-mm bead, one seed bead of color A, and four seed beads of color B. Using the needle-nose pliers, cut the end of the eye pin until it is ¼ inch long. Grasp the straight end of the eye pin with the tip of the pliers and make a loop.

The end of the eye pin should be touching the top of the last bead on the pin. Grasp the eye pin at the bottom of the loop and bend the eye pin down. This should open the loop, enabling you to slip the last link of one of the chain pieces onto the eye pin loop. Close the loop by gently pressing together with the pliers.

Make five more beaded eye pins and attach them to the cut pieces of chain. When you are finished you will have one long piece of chain connected by beaded eye pins, beginning and ending with chain. Place beads on another eye pin and attach to the free chain ends, closing the necklace. Place beads on the last eye pin and attach with jump rings to the eye pin that closed the necklace; the two eye pins will be parallel. Place beads on each head pin, close the loops, and, using jump rings to attach them, hang one beaded head pin from each end of the last eye pin.

Making loop on end of eye pin

Four-Bead Necklace

Simple and elegant, this necklace is an effective piece of jewelry that uses only a few elements.

Materials
4 large, interesting beads
28½ inches of heavy chain
3 1½-inch eye pins
1 1½-inch head pin
9 jump rings
Spring ring
Needle-nose pliers

Divide the chain into three sections, 17 inches, 3 inches, and 8½ inches long. If the chain is too heavy for the needle-nose pliers to cut, separate the links by prying them apart with the pliers. Using jump rings and eye pins, attach one bead to each end of the 8½-inch section. Attach the other two beads, one on the remaining eye pin and one on the head pin, to each end of the 3-inch section of chain. With a jump ring, attach the 3-inch section to the center link of the 17-inch section. Attach the ends of the 8½-inch chain section to the 17-inch section, 3½ inches to the right and 3½ inches to the left of the center. Attach a jump ring to one end of the 17-inch section and a jump ring and the spring ring to the other end.

Beaded Earrings

Beaded earrings are perhaps the easiest beaded items to make. Buy earring backs (either the screw type or the pierced-ear type) and attach beads that have been strung on wire, eye pins, or head pins. In less than an hour you can probably make enough different earrings to complement everything you wear or enough to make presents for everyone you know. Some of the earrings pictured here will inspire you to design your own.

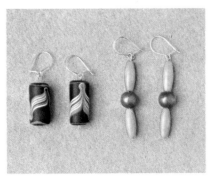

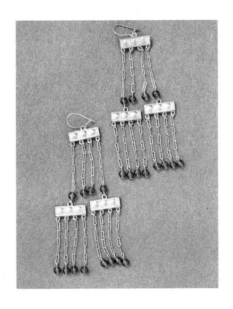

Beaded bags. From the collection of Diana Finegold.

Bibliography

Collum, Lurlene, *Bead and Pearl Jewelry*, Craft Course Publishers, Inc., Rosemead, California, 1971.

Edwards, Joan, *Bead Embroidery*, Taplinger Publishing Company, Inc., New York, New York, 1972.

Hofsinde, Robert, *Indian Beadwork*, The New American Library, Inc., New York, New York, 1958.

Hunt, W. Ben, and Burshears, J. F., *American Indian Beadwork*, The Bruce Publishing Company, New York, New York, 1951.

La Croix, Grethe, *Creating with Beads*, Sterling Publishing Company, Inc., New York, New York, 1969.

Wasley, Ruth, and Harris, Edith, *Bead Design*, Crown Publishers, Inc., New York, New York, 1970.

Weber, Betty J., and Duncan, Anne, *Simply Beads*, Western Trimming Corp., Culver City, California, 1971.

White, Mary, *How to Do Bead Work*, Dover Publications, Inc., New York, New York, 1972.

Suppliers

Unless stated otherwise, the following suppliers sell retail and mail order, and carry general beading supplies.

Bead Game
505 N. Fairfax Ave.
Los Angeles, Cal. 90036

Creative Craft House
910 St. Vincent Ave.
Santa Barbara, Cal. 93101

Earth Guild
149 Putnam Ave.
Cambridge, Mass. 02139

Glori Bead Shoppe
172 W. 4th St.
New York, N.Y. 10014

T. B. Hagstoz and Son
709 Sansom St.
Philadelphia, Pa. 19106
(tools; chain and findings in base and precious metals)

Jewelart Inc.
7753 Densmore Ave.
Van Nuys, Cal. 91406
(mail order only)

The Niddy Noddy
416 Albany Post Rd.
Croton-on-Hudson, N.Y. 10520

Plume Trading and Sales Co.
PO Box 585
Monroe, N.Y. 10950
(American Indian craft supplies)

Sax Arts and Crafts
PO Box 2002
Milwaukee, Wis. 53201

Terra-Cotta, Inc.
765 Massachusetts Ave.
Cambridge, Mass. 02139

Walbead, Inc.
38 W. 37th St.
New York, N.Y. 10018
(mail order only)

Lee Wards, Inc.
1200 St. Charles St.
Elgin, Ill. 60120
(mail order address)